I Wish for You
a *B*eautiful Life

I Wish for You a *B*eautiful Life

Letters from the Korean Birth Mothers
of Ae Ran Won to Their Children

edited by Sara Dorow
introduction by Mrs. Han Sang-soon

Yeong & Yeong Book Company
1368 Michelle Drive
St. Paul, Minnesota 55123-1459
www.yeongandyeong.com

Book design by Kim Dalros.

Front jacket painting © Kim Soo-ik.

Photography © Stephen Wunrow.

Publisher's Cataloging-in-Publication
(Provided by Quality Books, Inc.)

I wish for you a beautiful life : letters from the Korean birth
    mothers of Ae Ran Won to their children / edited by Sara Dorow ;
    introduction by Mrs. Han Sang-soon. -- 1st ed.
        p. cm.
        ISBN: 0-9638472-3-6

        1. Birthmothers--Korea (South)--Correspondence.
    2. Intercountry adoption--Korea (South) 3. Intercountry
    adoption--Psychological aspects.   I. Dorow, Sara.

    HV875.58.K67122 1999   362.82'98
                           QBI98-1344

Printed in the United States of America

06 05 04 03 02 01 00 99

This book is printed on acid-free paper.

To the Korean birth mothers,
and all adopted children and their families.

Introduction by Mrs. Han Sang-soon
Director of Ae Ran Won

When I first visited Minneapolis, Minnesota, my host was Brian Boyd of Yeong & Yeong Book Company. Spending that first evening together, we shared our thoughts about Korean birth mothers, and on our way back to Children's Home Society of Minnesota, we agreed to publish this book.

In Korea, there is much misunderstanding of birth mothers, as well as prejudice against them. They are often criticized for not showing responsibility for their babies and for being concerned only about their own well-being. It is thought that most of them are only interested in hiding their pregnancies, and that they go to the hospital to give birth with great fear. Some people look with contempt on those birth mothers who agree to send their babies away after a short counseling session with social workers from an adoption agency. These mothers often appear to be apathetic, almost numb, and they remain aloof from their problems, even denying them. Some young women just disappear from the hospital and, in some cases, if they can't find any help, they abandon their babies in the street, hoping that someone will find them and take care of them. I would like to emphasize that such behavior by birth mothers is a sign of even deeper conflicts than those of the young women who agonize about placing their babies for adoption. I believe that such behavior is defensive, and is the result of the scars and pain of the negative experiences in their lives, their unexpected pregnancies, and the shock of giving birth without any preparation. These feelings eventually lead them to think that they are helpless and alone. Furthermore, it is extremely difficult for the mothers to make proper judgments or display sensible behavior when they feel numb. That numbness is brought about by the shock and unforgettable sadness they experience. Along with this, I understand that it might be natural for the birth mothers to try to hide from the disapproving stares of society. I think their inability to cope and their subsequent desire to escape reality are the same as that of anyone who has to face an unbearable situation.

I wonder how they feel deep inside when the cold stares have faded away and the incident is all but forgotten by others. It is then that the wounds and suppressed emotions of grief, guilt and yearning surface again. It is precisely these feelings, if not treated properly, that cause much harm in their lives. On the other hand, if these feelings are treated properly and the mothers recover, I believe that they will be able to come out into the light from the darkness and make a new start.

We find that a helpful part of recovery is for each birth mother to express her feelings in the form of a letter to her child. It is my great pleasure to select some of these letters from our files at Ae Ran Won in order to share them with adopted children and their families. My staff and I hope that people who read these letters will better understand birth mothers, and we are honored that the profits from this book will benefit our work at Ae Ran Won. It is fitting that the stories courageously told by some birth mothers will help other women in their journeys.

Through this book I have wanted to share a clear picture of the reality of the unwed mothers and the indescribable pain that they undergo when they send their babies away for adoption. Furthermore, I would like to deepen the understanding of adopted children who grow up in foreign countries and in cultures different from Korea. I would like as best I can to help them answer the nagging question of "why." In doing so, I hope that their feelings of rejection will begin to heal.

I would like to thank the Lord, Our Father in Heaven, for allowing this book to be published. I also thank Brian Boyd, Sara Dorow, Maynard and Shirley Dorow, and many others who have given me much help and kind advice. In addition, I would like to thank my staff here at Ae Ran Won for their dedication, caring, and hard work. I especially thank Yeong & Yeong Book Company for donating profits from this book to Ae Ran Won to help Korean birth mothers. I would like to end with a prayer that God's blessings will reach everyone who helped achieve this result.

Han Sang-soon
Director of Ae Ran Won
Seoul, Korea
August, 1998

A Note from the Editor

Each of us has a story to tell. That this story is interwoven with the lives of other individuals and families is especially true for the adoptive family, whose story is not complete nor even possible without the story of the birth family. But the birth family's story may be inaccessible, poorly understood, or even avoided, leaving painful gaps in the adoption narrative.

The letters in this book were gathered with the intention of providing further access and understanding. Written by Korean birth mothers to their children, these letters offer a brief encounter with some very powerful stories and emotions. Full of the humanity, the hope, and the pain of women who have decided to place their children for adoption, these letters help lift some of the mystery we tend to drape around the "unknown" birth mother.

The story of a unique place called Ae Ran Won makes it possible to publish these letters. Ae Ran Won is an agency in Seoul that provides a temporary home to pregnant unmarried women before and after the birth of their children, and is one of few organizations in Korea that provide such support both during and after pregnancy.

I remember visiting the several one-room, tile-roof houses of Ae Ran Won when I was a child growing up in Korea. One stepped through the small gate into a simple courtyard, where kimchi jars were stacked to one side and fresh washing hung on a line to dry. Inside the main house there were usually nine or ten young women sitting on the heated ondol floor, using skills learned at Ae Ran Won to knit winter sweaters or embroider flower patterns, their conversation occasionally breaking the quiet. A large cross adorned one wall of the room.

Thirty years later, a new three-story facility stands next to the tiny original site. Its simple but comfortable accommodations for forty women are always full. The staff has grown to include a number of counselors and volunteers, and programs range from computer education to child care. Birth mothers' needs have changed as well. When Ae Ran Won was founded in 1960, its greatest concern was for the many young, vulnerable, and uneducated rural women migrating to the capital city in search of work. Several decades later the height of the mass urban migration is over, and South Korea has rapidly developed. Now the 200 or more birth mothers who stay at Ae Ran Won each year come with diverse backgrounds and needs, but they are all unmarried, pregnant, and looking for a supportive environment. They are fortunate to find Ae Ran Won. Its program of support, counseling, and education for birth mothers is a rare gem in a society that places a great deal of shame on single mothers.

During her few months at Ae Ran Won a woman receives education and counseling as she makes difficult decisions about her own and her child's futures. A few women—usually about 15 percent—decide they are able to raise their children. But given the overwhelming stigma of single motherhood and discrimination against children without legally recognized fathers, a young woman will in most cases choose adoption for her child. Within a day or two after delivery, she relinquishes her infant to one of a number of adoption agencies that work with Ae Ran Won.

Counselors at Ae Ran Won encourage each birth mother to write a letter to her child as one step toward working through this painful and sometimes numbing decision. These letters are kept on file at Ae Ran Won. Mrs. Han Sang-soon, Director of Ae Ran Won, recognized a unique opportunity to share some of the stories birth mothers have to tell. She wisely and generously made these letters available to a wider audience.

This material was more difficult to organize than one might imagine. We wanted the letters to speak for themselves—for the voices of birth mothers simply to be heard. For that reason, the letters were translated as directly as possible and edited only to protect confidentiality. But reading is a complex act of interpretation involving far more than simple words, particularly for material as emotionally and culturally laden as are these letters. We strive for a balance between voice and context. The letters are grouped around themes, and each group is preceded by a short introduction that helps provide context for the voices we hear in the letters.

Adopted persons and adoptive parents, especially those who want to share this book with their children, should read the Foreword by experienced social workers Maxine Walton and Jeff Mondloh before reading the letters. Readers are also invited to learn more about Ae Ran Won by reading the information provided in the back of the book. Let these letters also be an inspiration to continue reading and learning about Korea and Korean life.

These letters are a precious and complex gift from Ae Ran Won. They contain a variety of messages, and cannot possibly answer all of the many questions adopted persons and their families have. But the stories told in these letters, shared with honesty and courage, open up a space in which we can begin to understand the feelings and experiences of birth mothers. And they carry the vitally important message that birth children are remembered and cherished.

Sara Dorow
August, 1998

Foreword by Jeff Mondloh and Maxine Walton

Children's Home Society of Minnesota

I Wish for You a Beautiful Life is an invaluable gift to parents and children whose lives have been joined through Korean adoption. The book's personal letters chronicle the struggles that birth mothers face, the thoughts they have while making an adoption plan, and the journey they may follow as they ponder their few available options. These letters introduce the birth mothers' hopes and dreams for their birth children's future and present a unique perspective that has been elusive for adults, and even more so for children.

How might one use this book of letters? Initially, we thought of the interest children would have in reading about birth mothers' thoughts of hope, their commitment, and their messages of caring that shine through these letters. The letters allow a child's birth mother to become "real," yet they also contain life's struggles, disappointments, regrets, and lost dreams.

We strongly encourage parents to read and become familiar with these letters. Not once, but many times. By becoming familiar with the birth mothers' thoughts and feelings, parents of young children may find select quotes that help them anticipate and address the many questions children have about birth mothers. As children grow, the letters may be re-read and used to help normalize adoption and the birth mother's decision-making process. For parents of mature teens—youth who are able to understand the inconsistencies of life and separate their lives from the stories of the birth mothers—the letters may help address the sensitive questions involved in planning an adoption.

These letters express the birth mothers' innermost thoughts and feelings during a very emotional time in their lives. Words that the birth mothers use to express what is happening to them may not be sensitive to an adopted person's feelings or needs. The letters should be considered within a context. They capture an emotional whirlwind bridging the pregnancy, birth, and transfer of parental responsibilities that are experienced by birth mothers. For example, it is normal for Korean birth mothers' letters to convey feelings of guilt and sinfulness for having an unplanned pregnancy and making an adoption plan. However, it is not beneficial for children to think that they caused these feelings for the birth mothers.

The same is true of thoughts expressed by birth mothers about abortion or suicide. From a birth mother's perspective, it would not be unusual for her to consider these alternatives before making a commitment to continue her pregnancy. Understanding these topics takes exceptional emotional maturity. Parents will need to decide when it is appropriate to discuss these issues with their children. They are best equipped to select those quotes or passages that best express what their children need to hear at any given time.

I Wish for You a Beautiful Life is a useful tool in understanding the birth mothers' experiences. Yet its usefulness doesn't stop there. We hope that these stories will touch you in a way that would allow an exchange of information to take place. Korean adoption agencies are witnessing an increase in the number of birth parents who seek information about the health, welfare, and family of the child for whom they have made an adoption plan. Korean agencies have begun to facilitate requests for information on behalf of the Korean birthgiver.

We encourage families to update both the agency through which you adopted, and also the Korean agency, with a letter and photo. The letter can include identifying or non-identifying information depending on your family's preference. In this way, knowledge of your family and your feelings about giving and receiving information are recorded. Then if the birth mother should ever contact the Korean agency, the record would reflect the updated information about your family, which could then be passed to them. (Prior to sending an updated letter or requesting any other service of either the placing agency or the adoption agency in Korea, be sure to contact them to inquire about current policies, practices, and procedures that may apply to your requested services. The agencies will be able to clarify their ability to assist you with your request for further information or direct contact with the birth parents.)

As your child grows, it is important to have access to whatever additional information can be gleaned from the Korean agency's records. Efforts to make a personal connection with someone from the child's past can be equally important. The Korean social worker, foster care provider, orphanage director, or the person who initially found the child may provide some understanding of the child's life before he or she joins the adoptive family. A maternity clinic, police station, or site where the child was found can also be instrumental in helping children connect with their early beginnings. These efforts help focus on what is known of a child's early life. This interest becomes important for people at different stages of their lives.

It may be useful for parents to locate professional guidance when considering how to add to the child's background information or seek communication with birth families. Parents and children can only benefit from a greater understanding of how Korea's cultural traditions continue to impact birth mothers and adoption. For example, women who have had an unplanned pregnancy continue to keep this fact secret. They realistically fear that their family will shun them, marriage will not be possible, or their current marriage will end, and opportunities for self-advancement will be severely restricted. The same stigma extends to children raised by single parents. They are subjected to considerable teasing, and have little opportunity for a good education, marriage, or occupation. In a society which demands that all rites of passage include examination of the family register, it is not possible to keep your parentage private.

In many instances the Korean agency may not be able to add to the personal facts of one's birth ancestry. However, information about how service was given at the time of your family's adoption helps to frame the experience and give it greater depth and meaning.

The voices of Korean birth mothers can be heard clearly in the letters of *I Wish for You a Beautiful Life*. There is much to be gained by listening closely to what they say.

Jeffrey Mondloh ACSW, LICSW
Korean Program Director

Maxine Walton MS, LICSW
Counseling Program Supervisor

Post Adoption Services Department
Children's Home Society of Minnesota
2230 Como Avenue
St. Paul, MN 55108

The stigma of single motherhood

While traditional Korean values are undergoing steady change, the stigma against single parenthood remains stronger than perhaps we in the West can imagine. Bearing a child outside of marriage brings shame to the birth mother, her child, and her immediate and extended families. The deep embarrassment that accompanies pregnancy and parenthood out of wedlock is not just about immoral conduct but about disrupting traditional Confucian family bonds and a male-centered lineage. When a child has no legal father, a fact easily discerned from the all-important family register, both birth mother and child face social discrimination throughout their lives. In most cases they risk losing family ties and thus a social and financial safety net. They may also sacrifice prospects for marriage or a sustainable livelihood. Thus the women who write these letters are deeply torn. General social pressure, and in some cases specific pressure from family, leads many women to choose adoption. Some feel they had no choice but adoption, while others express that this was the best choice under the circumstances.

"*I love you, my dear baby.*"

The day you were born was a very difficult but happy time.
When I heard your cry at 11:30 P.M., I was looking at you with
so much joy in my heart. While I looked at you I felt so weak;
you were the most important part of me. You were so adorable
when you cried. Although I am the naive mother who bore
you, I wonder who will raise you and take care of you.

I love you very much.

I also loved you very much as you developed in my womb.
I whispered, "I love you, my dear baby" whenever I felt you in
my womb. I was grateful to you whenever you stirred so gently
in my womb because it felt as if you were looking after me.
When you were in my womb you liked fruit a lot, and also

meat. Actually, all types of food seemed to agree with you. After sleeping with you at night and waking up in the morning, your presence became very important to me.

Although your name was given after you were born, it was given to you with a wish that you would grow up with a pure heart, like a clear blue sky. Your birth father also knows your name because your name was chosen and given to you by both of us.

My dear son, please remember that I will always love you very much. I also want you to remember that you are my son and are very important to me. I remember like it was yesterday the way that you used to fall asleep. I miss you more and more as the days go by, and my heart aches.

But my dear son, I had to choose adoption because of the circumstances, which did not allow me to raise you at the time.

I hope that you will understand your mother. And please remember that I love you very much . . .

I hope God will guide your life and draw you to a close walk with Him.

To my son, whom I love very much.

"*From far away I will pray for your happiness.*"

My dear princess,

You may call this letter a personal history of your mother, who can never be forgiven by you.

I am twenty-seven years old. I am the eldest in my family of two girls and one boy. After I graduated from high school, I studied hairdressing and am now working as a hairdresser.

I committed such an unforgivable sin against you. There is nothing I could possibly say by way of an excuse, but I would like to write to you a little. If you can just understand me for having had to send you away. You are such an adorable baby to me, and I feel like my heart is tearing apart.

Your father lacked independence. He was a person who did not put words into action. I could not depend on him for the rest of my life, and so we had to go our separate ways. However, I decided not to blame or hate him because he is the one who gave life to you and loved you. I just take this as my fate.

When I found out that I was pregnant, I was overjoyed. Yet at the same time I began to worry, because I got pregnant before I was married to your father. I was afraid of how my parents would react. I was very scared and worried about the whole thing. One day I even decided to go to a hospital to have an abortion, but I did not have the courage to do it. I finally decided to keep you. After I made that decision, I felt peace in my heart.

As you were growing in me and as I felt you moving inside of me, I realized the importance and the mystery of life. I was so thankful that you were healthy. After twelve long hours of labor pain, you were born at 7:10 A.M. When I saw you for the first time, I totally forgot about all the labor pain I had been through. You turned the mystery of life into reality for me.

Your angel-like face while sleeping, your sneezing, your crying, your resemblance to your father, your little hands and feet, your pink fingernails, eyebrows, nose, lips—all those things looked so lovely and pretty. You were such a pretty princess. But now I have to say good-bye.

I reproached myself for being so bad, and cried with my heart aching and tearing apart. I thought about raising you by myself, but it would be hard, especially in Korea where the Confucian ideas are deeply rooted in society. So I decided to send you to meet good parents who could make you happy. I was in agony and despair, but now I have decided to live just praying for you.

I do not have any excuses for all these things, even though you might hate me to the end. I do not have anything to say other than that I am sorry. I am truly sorry.

Wherever you end up, I hope you will grow up to be a happy, healthy, kind, and beautiful woman. I would like to ask you to be responsible for your given tasks, and respect others. At the same time, voice your opinion with dignity so that you may overcome any difficulties in your life.

Finally, I will not ask you to forgive me, the one who had to send you away like this. I just wish that someday, when you get to be the age of a mother, you can understand me. From far away I will pray for your happiness, my beautiful princess.

Good-bye.

"*I* would buy a pair of red shoes for your feet."

To my daughter, whom I love,

I cannot bear the thought of not seeing you when I imagine that somewhere you may be crying. You were born by Caesarian section. After I woke up from surgery I was able to see you once but I cannot remember your appearance very well. I try very hard to remember what you look like but it becomes difficult and sometimes I have to give up.

My loving daughter, when I first felt you within me I dreamt of many things. One dream was about red shoes. When my mother, your grandmother, was raising me, she had hoped to buy me a pair of red shoes. I guess at the time, because of her poverty, it was too difficult for her. My mother, your grandmother, passed away before she could do this for me.

When I knew that you would be born, I dreamt that after your birth I would buy a pair of red shoes for your feet and a pretty ribbon with lace to put in your hair. However, now I cannot hug you or buy you the red shoes or even buy you a ribbon, and I am very sad. At first I couldn't accept this reality because I was so sad, but then I realized that you will have good adoptive parents. I believe they will be able to buy you the red shoes and ribbon, because you are like an angel given by God!

Daughter, even if I cannot see you or hug you right now because we are so far apart, I believe that you will grow up to be a cheerful and happy child. Let us always depend on God and we will meet each other in our hearts.

Your mother

letter 4

"_P_lease live your life with confidence."

To my darling daughter,

I don't know how I can express my feelings right now! My heart is torn apart because I could not keep you but had to give you up for adoption. You may blame me, but with time I hope you will understand. I did not want to give you up but I had no choice. When I signed the waiver of parental rights I was in tears of great agony. I hope by reading this letter you will know how much I loved you and how I did not want to give you up.

I was born in a very happy family, but when I was in third grade in elementary school tragedy came upon us. My father, your maternal grandfather, died of skin cancer. And my mother, your maternal grandmother, left home. My grandmother then took care of us three children. At one time I blamed my mother, but now I do not blame her anymore.

When I first gave birth to you, and then gave you up for adoption, my heart was broken and I was in tears every day. I just did not want to give you up like that. I knew that my mother left us because she did not have any choice, and although I did not abandon you, I also had no choice but to place you for adoption. I want to emphasize this to you.

When you grow up maybe you will understand my heart. If I had kept you, you might have blamed me when you grew up because you were born of a mother who had no husband. You might have blamed me, or given up on life, or hung around with a bad crowd. That would have been laying a worse burden on you, and I could not let that happen.

Dear baby, despite these facts, please live your life with confidence. Do not think of me, but in rough times depend in all things on the Lord Jesus and walk with Him that you may become a great person. Only that will make me very happy, and it will benefit your future as well. I wish one more thing, and that is that you will do only what pleases God.

Good-bye, then.

Your loving mother

"*This* was the best way for you and me to be happy."

My beloved child,

A blue sky, trees and mountains, and singing birds that fly in the sky were all there as if to celebrate a baby's birth. My heart was among them and my mind was quite at ease.

I was not old enough to be pregnant, but I was ready to deliver my baby. What could I say when I met my baby? In a swirl of many words I was dispirited, and I cried.

When the person who was in charge of my baby brought you and left you beside me, I cried again. Why did I give birth to you and then have to place you with others? I hated myself. And I hated the person who showed you to me only that one time. Just like that, we were separated.

My sweetheart!

Good-bye.

My darling baby!

I wanted to keep you, but your grandmother didn't agree with me.

My darling baby!

It was not easy to say good-bye.

However, as your grandma said, this was the best way for you and me to be happy.

My darling! Be happy.

My sweetheart! Be healthy.

I hope you won't have to suffer the kind of pain I have suffered. Can I see you when you become an adult? How dare I see you again, sinner that I am!

I can endure anything if it is for your happiness, my dear. I can endure anything if it is for your good future. As my mother used to say, this is the way for you . . .

Please be happy, honey!

Letting you go with love

"*I* wish for God's blessing upon you in the future."

This is a time when my heart aches, thinking about the past.

I was not outgoing, did not mingle with others very well, and enjoyed times by myself, thinking about happiness. I was petite, confident about my looks, and born in a wealthy family. The world may not understand me, someone who grew up with all the things and all the love that I needed.

Because of my carelessness, I bore a child that I was not able to raise and had to deal with much pain. I did not feel blessed like other people do when they have a baby.

At the beginning I spent all my time choosing either to die or to get an abortion. The time passed so quickly while I was trying to decide. Consequently, I ended up in this situation.

Knowing the importance of prenatal care, I used my time to read books and devoted myself to you. I spent many nights thinking about what kind of person you would become in the future or who your adoptive parents would be, and hoping that you would grow up healthy and happy.

Even during my long labor pains, I thought much about whether I could send you away. When I saw your face and heard you cry for the first time at the end of my labor—Ah, I thought, I had to raise this child. But the thought floated away like a bubble.

How can I pity myself with the pain of sending you away? I just had to understand my future. Can you understand this? I had to give you up as soon as you were born, my lovely child, because I loved you so much. Maybe you will hate me.

But I had to send you away because I was sending you to a better environment and a better place where you could be happy rather than live with an incompetent mother. It may sound like an excuse, but it would be too cruel to raise you as the child of a single unwed mother in this society because of the way people would treat you.

Whenever I see children on the street, I go crazy. Everything weighs on my heart, and it hurts that I could not peacefully hold you nor lie down next to you—not even once.

Dear baby! My baby! I wish for God's blessing upon you in the future.

"*Your* beautiful cries made me so happy."

My darling boy,

I don't know where to begin, my loving child. First of all, I'd like to ask for your sincere forgiveness. I don't know when you will be able to read this letter, but I'd like to believe that you will forgive your mother.

My son, I decided to tell you the whole truth about your birth.

I met your daddy in June, 1990 and we fell in love with each other within a short time. The month after we met, we started to live together in a small house in Kyung-gi province and I became pregnant right away. I was so happy for you during that time. I believed that you were a gift from God. I had only good thoughts for you and tried to eat nutritious food for my baby.

Unfortunately, your daddy didn't trust that you were his baby and he tried to force me to have an abortion. What an absurd idea this was!

Finally, I had to move back to my parents' house while carrying you in my body. Your grandmother and grandfather also tried to force me to have an abortion. I was so sad and distressed. I had to hide myself from my parents to keep you and didn't go back to their house until I was seven months pregnant. I thought they might have given up their thoughts because it was too late to have an abortion. However, they pressured me as before and I had to suffer many things.

My dear! I am telling you all these stories, not because I want to tell about my suffering, but because I want to tell how dearly I loved you and wanted you.

My darling son, you also have your grandfather and grandmother on your father's side, living in another province. They are nice people. They wanted you and asked me to bring you to their home. But they could not afford to raise a baby, so I decided not to let you go to their place.

As the delivery day approached, my stomach became larger and larger and it became uncomfortable to move. I was so afraid but didn't know what to do. I didn't have a delivery plan and didn't have money to go to the hospital to deliver you. My parents also didn't have money to afford it. I was so distressed. Your daddy didn't show up at all, and I was led to Ae Ran Won.

You were born sixteen days early at 1:50 P.M., in healthy condition. Not even remembering the labor pains, I was so happy that you were born healthy and safe. Your beautiful cries made me so happy. When I saw you for the first time, I could tell you looked exactly like your daddy—sharply shaped eyes, evenly-arranged eyelashes, clearly shaped nose, and thin lips. Only your dark hair was like me. Your body shape was like your daddy, too. However, your daddy didn't trust me. What nonsense . . .

The more I watched you, the more deeply the love in my heart arose. You are the very son whom I kept in my body for nine months under all those difficulties! I was so happy for you during the time we had together after your birth.

However, my happy times were too short and a social worker from the adoption agency came to take you away from me. She asked me several questions regarding relinquishment of parental authority. After that, she dressed you up and covered you with a pretty comforter. Then she held you in her arms and you instinctively looked at your mommy. I could hardly watch the scene and felt carried away by the pain in my heart.

My darling!
I am sorry, my dear baby, please forgive me.
You left me that way and I am very sorry.
Forgive me. My heart is still torn.

My baby!
I had prenatal care when I was pregnant.

I dreamed that my baby would be a sincere person and a good Christian.

I pray for you every day.
Be a happy and lovable person.

I named you, my baby.
My darling baby, I dearly love you.
Please forgive your foolish mother.

Love,
Your mother

The adoption decision

As some of these letters indicate, social stigma combines with other circumstances to lead to the decision to adopt. Once that decision is made, a birth mother may request that her child be placed in Korea or internationally. All of these writers want the best for their children, but knowing what is "best" is very difficult. A birth mother might ask that her child be placed with a Korean family, perhaps finding comfort in the fact that her child will remain in familiar cultural and racial surroundings. But other factors weigh into this decision as well. An adopted person often is not accepted into Korean society, and may never know that he or she was adopted. Not only is adoption of a non-relative a new and strange concept for many Koreans, for whom blood ties are very important, but open adoption is nearly impossible. If a birth mother places her child domestically, in almost every case she will have no further contact with the child and adoptive family.

A birth mother might choose international adoption because of the possibility of seeing her child again, a sentiment expressed in a number of letters. She might also believe her child will face less discrimination and greater opportunity as an adopted person in a Western country. The difficulty of this decision lies in placing a great distance between herself and her child, and between her child and his or her Korean heritage.

"How adorable you were from the moment of your birth!"

My dear loving son,

It is hard for me to write this letter. I have lots of stories to tell you, but I don't know how to start. I hope you will remember that every decision I made, I made for you. I don't think the reason that I placed you for adoption was because I didn't love you. It was really a hard decision for me, but I think my decision was right for you. Please don't forget that I love you. I'll love you and worry about you forever. Nothing can change my mind about you.

First let me tell you something about your father and me. I met your daddy when I was in trouble. He was, too. We met each other when we both badly needed someone, and we fell in love. We spent a wonderful time together, and the most beautiful thing happened—your birth. Unfortunately, I should have realized that the time we had and the love we shared were an empty dream. Our love was not enough for us to make a beautiful life together. I wished that all the problems I faced were not real. But I have no regrets. I was happy for you, and I still am. I believe time can cure everything.

I was only able to meet you when I was in the hospital. You were the most beautiful baby I have ever seen. How adorable you were from the moment of your birth! Your chubby cheeks were rose colored, and your distinctive and sensitive facial expression was so mysterious to me. You were such a good baby while you were with me. Whenever I went to the nursery to see you, you looked so comfortable even though other babies were crying. You weren't fussy or irritable. Whenever I fed you, you slept as if you were not hungry at all. You loved to sleep, and I worried that you inherited that from me because I love to sleep.

As your mother I was always concerned about you. There was no way for us to live together. I gave birth to you, so I had the responsibility to provide a wonderful environment for you. I preferred to say good-bye to you rather than to live with you, if that decision could bring you better opportunities. And that's why I decided to place you with others. Looking into adoption, I realized that you would get something that I could not provide—a family. You needed to be loved by family members, and you could have that love only if you were in a family. I couldn't give that love by myself. Therefore, adoption was my gift to you. I wished for you to have many opportunities. I believe you have those opportunities now.

I hope you will always remember how fortunate you are. Isn't it good to have wonderful parents who love you as I do? Even though I can't meet you, in spirit I am always with you, and my love will never fade away. I envy your parents because they are with you and can share joy and sorrow with you. Nevertheless, I thank God that you are a part of me, and that I could spend three days with you after your birth. I'll remember you forever.

I don't know how well I am expressing the thoughts and feelings that I wanted to share with you. But I am happy to have this chance to talk to you about your daddy and myself. My son, respect yourself always, and respect others, too. Never put yourself down or underestimate yourself. Do your best in whatever you do. Do not be afraid of making mistakes, because people can learn from mistakes. There are a lot of people around you; ask them for help if you need it. Remember that you are not alone, because you have a family. I think you will read this letter someday and will be able to find me. I'll welcome you anytime. Even though I wish to meet you someday, it is up to you. Nobody can force you to do something you don't want to do. If you are happy, I am happy. I'll accept and understand any decision that you make.

My son, you are always part of me, and I am proud of you. My love will always be with you. I hope your days will be full of joy, and good luck to you.

Love,
Your mom, who will love you forever

"*You* were born of our love and I will love you forever."

My darling baby,

Hello, darling. I hope you are healthy and growing up well. Today is a gloomy autumn afternoon and the weather is pretty cold in the morning and at night. As usual my thoughts turn to you and your health.

My baby, I am writing this letter with a great longing for you. From early on I realized the importance of life, and love for you started to bloom in my heart. My precious baby, who wriggled in my body for nine months . . . You were part of me, and now I've been without you for a month. Each day has been torture for me and I've had to suffer from guilt. I would like to put an end to my past grievous life and start a new life from now on.

My precious baby, I don't know if I am worthy of being called "mother." Also, I am afraid to say "forgive me" as I don't deserve to be forgiven by you.

I liked music very much. I loved the piano, its sound, and a man who played the piano. Your daddy was a piano teacher. He also loved me and I became pregnant. However, he was a married man, so I couldn't tell him that I was pregnant. I decided to have an abortion and went to the hospital. But the doctor said that it was too late and he recommended that I go to Ae Ran Won, a shelter for unwed mothers. While staying at Ae Ran Won, I regretted my foolish thoughts about aborting a precious life.

My baby, you were born after eleven hours of labor, and you were the most adorable princess to me. How I wished to be with you until the end of my life. But I couldn't do that because I didn't want my princess to live with constant rudeness from others. Also, I couldn't provide a good home for you, and I didn't want to transfer my poverty to you. I wanted you to grow up full of love.

My sweetheart, I went out today in a gloomy mood. I watched happy women along the streets holding their babies. I envied them and burst into tears from missing you so much. My darling, I am turning over a new leaf. That way I can show my happy life to you when you become an adult and visit me in the future. You were born of our love and I will love you forever.

I miss you so much! I have been lucky lately in that I can meet you in my dreams very often. I then wake up the next morning soaked with perspiration and even more anxious to see you. It is so difficult to express all my feelings with this letter.

My beloved princess! I hope you will grow up to be healthy, strong, and beautiful. Good-bye.

From your loving mother

P.S. I'll pray that you meet the most wonderful parents.

"*My* love for you will continually grow."

My baby, what can I say to you . . . I fear that you will not believe what I have to say. I do hope that you will believe me when I say that I love you, my daughter. I know that no matter what I say I cannot be forgiven, but I hope that you will come to understand me a little.

My baby, when you grow up you may ask why your mother gave you up for adoption abroad. You may think that if you had grown up in Korea and had been adopted by a Korean family, you would not have gone through so much hardship. However, when I was faced with the decision of giving you up for adoption I believed that you would be better off in a country where you would be given an equal chance.

The reason I did not give you up for domestic adoption was that children adopted in Korea, even if they are not born out of wedlock, are discriminated against and looked down upon. Even if your adoptive parents tried to keep the fact of your adoption a secret, eventually it would be revealed. When I considered how you would be shocked when you found out too late that you had been adopted, I had to decide that it would be best for you to be adopted abroad.

My baby, if you understand me a little, I hope that you will realize that I want you to love your adoptive parents. Even though I am your biological mother, I could not provide you with the loving environment that you need. I admit that I was irresponsible. Your adoptive parents, even though they are not your biological parents, will care for you with all the love and attention they can give. What I also hope is that wherever you are, you understand that the Lord Jesus is with you and that you are a child of God. I hope that you will always have a positive attitude and high self-esteem, with healthy thoughts and a heart that cares for others as well.

I will never forget you but I will always pray for you. My love for you will continually grow.

I love you.

From your loving mother

"I will always live with you in my heart."

When I call your name I feel pain in my heart because you are so young and your adoptive parents may be the only people in your life right now. Even though I gave you life and gave you your name I could not keep you because of hard circumstances beyond my control. I chose adoption for you despite the anguish that I feel and despite the fact that you may not understand why I did so.

I am very sorry. I cannot help crying when I think of you and remember what you look like. I could have given you all the love you needed from the moment I gave you birth as your mother, but because of the circumstances I was in we could only spend a short time together. Our relationship as mother and child, even though I wanted it to continue, ended so quickly because I had no other choice.

When I first looked into your face I tried to see what features we had in common. Knowing that it would be our last time together, my heart ached because as your mother I could not do anything for you.

When I looked into your face I knew that I would never forget you until the day of my death. Placing you in the care of adoptive parents was the most difficult thing for me, but when I think that they will provide you with happiness and that you will provide them with happiness as well, then I feel relieved.

Dear baby, I hope you will be loved by your family and grow up to be a healthy, strong, and great person. Later on when you find out that you are an adopted child (even though in my heart I hope that you will not know, because I don't want people to treat you differently) you may search for me.

Until that possible future meeting, I hope that I will live my life with confidence, trying to do my best in all that I do. I will also try my best to help you understand why my heart aches when I think of the fact that you were given up for adoption, even though you were not at fault in any way. But I should stop thinking in this way, because you were not given up but merely taken care of by different parents. I will consider you a gift to them and they will help you to grow up as a fine person.

Your mother loves you very much and has not given you up forever. I have chosen this way because I believe it is best for you. I will always pray for you and live with you in my heart. I hope that you will grow up healthy.

"*How* could you know the pain in my heart?"

To my baby,

Thinking of you living under the same sky and on the same earth as me, I miss you. I do not know what I should say, or how I should say it. Even though I am ashamed of myself, I want to be called your mother, at least before you go to your new parents.

When I had to send you away at the hospital, I reproached myself for being so powerless and irresponsible. I do not know how many times I had to bite my lip to endure the pain that was tearing at my heart.

But that pain never ends. I lie down day and night with my eyes wide open, just thinking about you. Many times I have picked up the phone and hung it up again, hesitating to call the adoption agency just to get your picture. But I think that seeing your face would leave me even more reluctant to give you up.

Maybe I wanted to make up for my irresponsibility, so I thought about what I could do for you.

After a lot of consideration, I found the answer. I realized that the best thing I can do is pray for your obedience to God and for your future health and happiness.

A day began to seem like a year, and I condemned myself so many times. But remember this: though you are far away, you remain imprinted on my heart like a picture, like a personal seal.

My dear child, how could you know the great pain in my heart? When you grow up and you realize that people around you are different from you, and that you were abandoned, you will face a lot of difficulties. That hurts me even more.

But if I condemn myself more, will my burden be lighter?

I still clearly remember holding you in my arms in the hospital. Sometimes I still cry when I think of your little hands like delicate fern leaves, your small lips, your soft skin. But from now on, I will be praying for you with gladness rather than sorrow.

I will pray that you meet a bright future, brighter than the summer sun that agonized me. I hope that you will be a very handsome, fine man wherever you are.

_A_ variety of voices

Although all birth mothers face social stigma, no one story can sum up the diverse experiences of the women who write these letters. Their letters tell of their own varied life histories and of the many different events that surround their decision to adopt. It should also be noted that because Ae Ran Won serves only single women, a variety of voices are not heard in these letters. Many Korean birth parents are married, but decide they cannot adequately parent their infant or older children because of personal circumstances, poverty, or the inability to meet their children's medical needs. Also not included are the stories of parents whose children are of mixed racial heritage. Social stigma forces difficult decisions for these parents. Finally, although the stories of birth fathers remain largely untold, some women do introduce us to their relationships with birth fathers. It is important to keep in mind that Korea continues to have a strong Confucian patriarchal system in which male-female relations are often dictated by long-held norms about appropriate social role and status.

"I wish for you a beautiful life."

My darling and lovely baby,

I met your daddy in the cool of winter when there were no stars shining through the bare branches of the trees and a chilly wind was blowing. We sat in a cafe, drinking hot coffee and making sweet talk. I felt like the whole world was mine. He was handsome and 183 centimeters tall, so he was popular among women. But he loved only me, and our beautiful and precious love became deeper and deeper.

One hot muggy summer day, because I could not take a summer vacation, I was lying in my room in front of a fan. An old lady came to visit me. She was your daddy's mother. She strongly disagreed with our relationship because there was too much of a gap between our social and economic classes. Also, your daddy had to continue his studies. I couldn't meet your daddy again after that, and I couldn't reach him when I tried to inform him that I was three months pregnant.

My sweet and pretty baby, I needed money to have an abortion, so I worked in the kitchen of someone's house. Once I had earned some money, I went to the hospital and saw you through the ultrasound. After hearing the beating of your heart, seeing your features through the screen, and feeling your movement in my body, I just couldn't have an abortion. I realized that you were alive in my body, and I could not commit such an unpardonable sin. So I came back from the hospital.

As time went by, my stomach became large with you. I was so afraid and didn't know what to do. It was a desperate time in my life. Then I was led to Ae Ran Won, and I delivered the most adorable and pretty baby at 2 A.M. on a Monday morning.

My daughter! I bore you in suffering and pain, so I couldn't stop crying whenever I looked down at you lying next to me. I felt like the world was upside down. My sweetheart! You looked a lot like me. You had a cough when I sent you away and my heart was full, thinking about you. I couldn't bear the pain. I wailed for you in the corner of a dark room. Mother's love! That's what it is.

As the days pass, I yearn for these things:
   to hold you one more time . . .
   to feed you one more time . . .
   to meet you one more time . . .

My darling! You may never be able to forgive me. I won't ask you to forgive me because mine is the sin of giving up my own child. For what I did I am ready to accept any punishment, until the end of my life or forever.

I hope that you have met good parents and that you will have a good life. I wish for you a beautiful life, with a beautiful face and a beautiful heart. Think of your life as precious, because you are a beautiful flower born out of pain. I cannot give you any help, but I will always pray for you. I chose your name by myself. You will remain in my heart forever with this name. How much you must have grown. I wish you a life with God always.

Your loving mother

"*It* grieved me that I had to let you go."

My beautiful daughter,

I hesitated to write this letter because of guilt and regret. I know it is impossible for you to forgive me, but I would like to receive your forgiveness. You must be curious about your mother. Let me introduce myself to you.

I was born in a northern province and grew up there. I was raised with one older brother, one younger sister, and one younger brother. Our parents were wonderful to us and it was a happy home. We all liked music a lot, so we each played a musical instrument. We also sang very well, so we used to sing and give prizes among ourselves. Our neighbors envied our family and they called us a "music family." It was really a happy family.

Do you know what your mother's dream was, my baby? I wanted to be a famous fashion designer. Fashion design was part of the department of Domestic Science at the college, so I applied to the department. However, designing dresses and drawing the beauty of women's curved lines was hard for me. I tried my best but my impatient personality didn't allow my dream to come true.

I regret that my past experience had not exposed me to life's difficulties, so I became too easygoing a person. I disliked my personality, but it was too late for me to change it.

I met your father when I was a college student. We graduated from the same middle school. By coincidence we met again at college. We were just friends at the beginning of our relationship, but as time went on, we became lovers. I was afraid when our relationship went beyond friendship. And I disliked myself for not being able to control my relationship with him.

After graduating from college I took care of the housework because my parents were busy with their farm work. Doing the housework was good for me, since I didn't have to find an outside job to make a living. My friends envied my situation and I was content with my circumstances. Now I can say it was not real life, because people can grow through social experiences and conversations with others. During that time your father called me often and visited me when my parents weren't at home.

One day I visited your daddy's house and got a hearty welcome from his mother. I was very happy about it.

I visited his house one or two times and got approval regarding our future relationship from his sister and relatives. Your daddy was an only son in his family.

Knowing that my parents would not approve, I did not have confidence to approach them. Generally, my parents let me make my own decisions. However, they would not allow me to choose my husband on my own. I strongly insisted to my parents that I would marry your daddy. They even cried in front of me, they were so disappointed. It was the first time for me to see my parents' tears, so my heart was broken. I wavered between disobedience and love. Because of me a happy family atmosphere had turned to sorrow. Just at that time I realized that I was four months pregnant.

I went to the hospital and learned that I could have an abortion at four months, but I thought that would be a worse sin than disobeying my parents. I didn't tell anybody that I was pregnant and tried to hide myself from others. When I was nine months pregnant, one of my friends introduced me to Ae Ran Won, a place for unwed mothers. They helped me deliver my baby safely.

I had mixed feelings of joy and sorrow when you were born. I was happy that you were born safely, and I was sorry that I couldn't keep you. It grieved me that I had to let you go.

My baby! My heart is so broken as I write this letter. I feel more pain than at any time in my life. My darling, wherever you may go, I hope that you will be a pretty and lovely person. I hope that you will not let any difficult circumstances of life upset you but that you will be strong and will grow up as a respectable person.

Above all else, please forgive me. This is all that I ask.

Good-bye.

Your mother

"$\mathscr{I}$ know I am too young to be a mother."

My baby,

How are you, my darling? Your mother is only fourteen years old. I know I am too young to be a mother. But I gave birth to you, so I am your mother.

As I send you away, I have an earnest desire. It is that you will be healthy and happy with your adoptive parents, and that you will be a good daughter to them. You are very young now, but when you grow up and get to know all these things, please don't resent or hate me for them.

Listen carefully to what your birth mom has to say. I used to not take good care of myself and while wandering about, I was sexually assaulted and became pregnant with you as a result.

I was so afraid after that, so I did work that was tiring for a pregnant woman, and wished that I would die. I used to think about having an abortion. But I am happy for you now that you are born.

My darling baby, don't live like me. When you live with your adoptive parents, even though you should face hardships, be patient, work hard, and become a fine person.

I am glad that I can write this letter to you. Before writing this letter, the only heart I could show you was very lonely and gloomy.

My baby! I don't know when or where we might meet again. Please don't forget or reproach me, and please love me.

I am sorry . . .
Your mother

"*I* touched your cheeks and nose."

To my darling boy,

You were born at daybreak in August. What a beautiful sound your crying was! I will never forget that day, and recall it again as I write this letter to you.

I was the fourth child in a family of two boys and three girls. I grew up in the countryside and have a high school diploma. Now I work with computers for a living.

Your daddy worked at a construction company and then served in the army. We loved each other and we still love each other. I was very happy when I heard that I was pregnant for the first time. I decided that I would be the best mother and raise my baby to be a healthy and wonderful person. I also decided that I would do my best to overcome all my difficult circumstances.

However, the realities of my life were beyond my control, and I had to go to the hospital for an abortion. I felt I would rather die than have an abortion, and I cried bitter tears. I couldn't go through with the abortion and came back home.

I had lived through so much anguish. By giving birth to you, my long journey of pain and agony was over. You and I lay down side by side on the bed of the delivery room, and I sobbed. You were such an adorable baby, with shining eyes, a cute nose, and little tiny lips. You looked exactly like your daddy. The look on your face when you cried, your two fists tightly clenched, is as vivid in my mind as a movie. I miss you so much.

I did all that I could for you but things did not work out as I had hoped. Rather, I even hated and resented you. But I cannot say such things to you and I only want to say that I am sorry. We met for only three hours, and I wanted to convey all my love to you. I touched your cheeks and nose while crying, but you smiled and were happy.

Shortly after that, you left me without so much as turning to look back, and I was hurt by your seeming indifference. But then, all my suppressed grief and pain welled up and I cried myself out. Although we were apart, I wanted to say that I am your mother and you are my son.

My loving son! I believe you are healthy and happy wherever you are. I hope you will be a nice boy who can live by sound judgment. I hope we can be proud of each other if we ever meet when you are an adult and I am forty-one, not twenty-one. I'll do my best to be a mother whom you can be proud of. I hope you can grow to be a son I will be proud of as well.

I love you, my precious little treasure.

Good-bye.

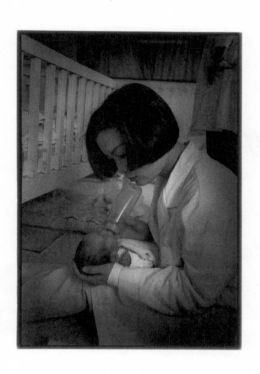

" *What a wonder life is.* "

My darling, my other self,

When I knew that I was pregnant, I worked hard to choose just
the right Chinese characters to make you a beautiful name. It
took a lot of pain and tears for me to keep you in my body.
However, I tried to listen to good music, enjoy pretty scenery,
and keep my mind and thoughts on prenatal care. I hope your
hate and reproach will be lighter after reading this letter.

Don't you want to know about your father? I was the only
daughter to your grandmother. She raised me for seventeen
years after your grandfather died when I was a small child. I
couldn't agree with my mother's second marriage, so I ran
away to my aunt's house. After that I went to Seoul to find a
job and was hired at a small manufacturing firm. I was known

as a hard-working and enthusiastic worker, so I was quickly promoted and had good standing in the company. During that time, I met a man through business relationships. He was a considerate man and was so kind to me. He gave me good advice when I encountered hard times. One day I realized that I was in love with him. When I couldn't see him, I missed him a lot. It was truly a mystery that in my nineteen years I had never had such feelings.

We loved each other for three years. Whenever we had a fight or a crisis during that time, your father smoothed over our differences. That is how you were conceived. I was so happy, but my sadness was just as great.

Your daddy was the eldest son in his family. According to his family tradition he was obliged to meet with a woman (not me) with a view to arranging a marriage. But for whatever reason, despite only being engaged to this woman, they were living together. Moreover, he had a two-year-old son from the relationship. He tearfully told me this whole story after hearing the news of my pregnancy, and I felt betrayed. After that, we broke up. I thought about having an abortion, but I didn't. My circumstances became worse and worse as time went by, so I went to the hospital. The doctor introduced me to Ae Ran Won, and I delivered you after staying at Ae Ran Won for one week.

What a wonder life is, and what a marvel that you arrived after I passed through deep pain and sorrow. You looked exactly like your daddy, and that reminded me of my past struggle. I couldn't keep my eyes off of you from the first time we met to our last moment of farewell. You were so adorable and marvelous I could hardly believe it. My heart ached for so long, I shed enough tears to make a flowing river.

My baby!

Do you think me cold-hearted and reproachable? If you see me someday, will you want to strike me? I share those feelings, my baby. I want to cry out loud. My sweetheart, can you see my tears? Can't you hear my weeping? My pains were so deep they were impossible to share with anyone in this world. I can never forget your beautiful features. I miss you so much. I am sorry to say this, but I even wished to die with you if it were possible.

I was consoled that you were a baby boy. People at the hospital said you were a gentle, bright, and sensitive baby boy, and I was so happy. Who knows? If you had been a baby girl, perhaps you would have lived like me . . .

From a great distance, I hope that in whatever environment you grow up, and whatever you may be, you will be both strong and humble. I pray with folded hands that you will be held in affection by others. It would be good for you to become a great tree, but I'm afraid that if you do you will not be a tender shoot like your father.

My darling! Once again I ask you to forgive me. Please try to understand me, understand my tears . . . My darling baby! I don't know where you will grow up, but please be a good son whom your parents will be proud of. I hope that you will grow up as a person who is obedient to his parents, respectful of his elders, and helpful to others.

I will cherish you in my heart forever. I love you and I miss you so much. Be healthy and happy. How much I wish to give you a big hug.

Well, it is time to say good-bye to you. I will always pray for you. Good-bye, and I love you.

Although a sinner, I will always pray for your happiness . . .

your mother

" *You* cried in a loud voice as if you knew your mother's heart."

My two dear angels,

I would have liked to write a letter earlier, but I wasn't doing well after delivery. Now I can greet you. Only God knows whether this letter is the first and the last letter between us.

I'd like to introduce myself first. I was born in 1956. After graduation from high school, I married a military officer. I have one son from that marriage. He is now fifteen years old. He is in the second year of middle school and is a good student. However, my husband had an affair and left us. I was twenty-four years old and your brother was three.

After that I lived singly, looking after your brother and maternal grandmother for twelve years. During that time I met a man, and he was your daddy. I thought he would be a good husband, and his family approved of our marriage. However, he left me without any notice when we were preparing for marriage. Just at that time I found out I was five months pregnant. I inquired into rumors trying to find your daddy, but in vain. After serious consideration, I decided to give birth to you.

I quit my job and focused on prenatal care while taking care of your brother and grandma. I also prayed for your health every day and tried to forgive your daddy.

When I was eight months pregnant, I moved into your aunt's house to hide myself from others. I got a lot of scolding for being pregnant, but I didn't care. I lived there and took care of your aunt's housework.

It was very early one morning when I felt the beginnings of labor. I prepared breakfast for the family, cleaned the house, and took a shower. Then I went to Ae Ran Won to get help with delivery.

You were identical twins, born five minutes apart. When you were born, I prayed: "Thank you Lord, for giving me these healthy babies. But what can I do since I can't keep them? I entrust these babies and their futures to you, Lord."

When I was praying, you cried in a loud voice as if you knew your mother's heart. We cried together. While crying, I gave you your names. I called the first baby Ha-na ("Number One"), the second Doo-ri ("Number Two").

I pray that you will be placed together in a wonderful home with wonderful parents. I think you should not be separated since you are twins. I will pray for this.

Please understand your mother. I dearly wanted to keep you, but I couldn't afford to. If your grandma were healthy, she could take care of you while I worked. However, her poor health doesn't allow her to take care of her grandchildren. I only pray for your good future.

My dear Ha-na and Doo-ri, Ae Ran Won is a place for unwed mothers like me. Women are supposed to stay for four weeks after delivery, but I decided to stay here for only a week. After recovering from childbirth, I will visit the place where you are staying. I will see you then.

Good-bye Ha-na and Doo-ri. If ever we are given the chance in the future, let's try to meet each other with happy minds and bright faces. Don't blame me because my heart is more bitter than yours. Please stay healthy, my dear Ha-na and Doo-ri. God bless you and be with you forever.

Your mother

Dear Parents of Ha-na and Doo-ri,

I would like to say something to you through this letter. Please provide good care and support to Ha-na and Doo-ri even though I could not. It is said that raising a baby has greater meaning than giving birth to a baby. Please raise these babies with prayer, in good times and in hard times. God bless you, and I am very sorry.

I'll always pray for you and your family.

Ha-na and Doo-ri's birth mom

$\mathcal{E}$ motion and fate

The complex emotions that surface for birth mothers throughout the process of birth and relinquishment are understandable. To the Western reader, however, the depth of feeling and style of expression in these letters may seem jarring. Koreans are passionate people for whom harboring and releasing emotions is very important. Feelings of shame and resentment are especially overwhelming when one's life situation is out of sync with social norms and thus causes embarrassment for others. In many of the letters, birth mothers pour out their feelings as a way of unburdening their guilt and restoring balance to their own and their children's lives.

In some cases the letters also refer to a sense of fate or destiny, which is a central idea in Korean thought. The course of a person's life is seen as not necessarily in her control. The sense of fate and emotion expressed in these letters may be heightened by the poignant weeks after relinquishment in which many of the letters were written. Moreover, the birth mothers sometimes employ what is common in Korean writing: a stylized and passionately poetic form of expression.

"*Sometimes we cannot do or act as we wish.*"

To my loving son,

It is very cloudy today and there was news of an approaching typhoon. It seems it will rain soon and the sky looks ominous.

Perhaps you don't know yet what the sky is or what rain is, but as you grow older you will learn of many things in this world that are beautiful and worthy of love. I hope that you will experience all these things as you grow and learn.

Yesterday when I saw your picture I cried a lot. I thought about wanting to see you as you sleep and also wanting to see you as you laugh. I even wanted to see you when you cry, and really every possible thing about you. I miss not seeing and experiencing these things. I can only imagine them, and what you look like, in my heart. I know that I have wronged you.

The day that you were taken away in the hospital I was not able to hug you even once, and that breaks my heart. I would give up everything that I have just to have been able to hug you once. But I cannot change anything now.

Oh, how much I wavered about this decision to place you for adoption, especially after sending you off like that. You were inside me for nine months and then I had to give you up to a stranger just a few hours after you were born. I realized what a terrible thing that was only after I had given you up.

If only I had known how you would be taken away so easily and quickly, I would have been a little bit more prepared by embracing you after your birth. Now that I have sent you away I wonder how I will be able to live the rest of my life.

But know this one thing—that even if you are brought up by someone else you will always be my baby and I will always have a longing for you. I will continually pray for you and wish for only good things to happen to you. Even if we cannot live as a mother and her loving baby I still love you very much. Please forgive me for my irresponsibility and for giving you up, but know that it was not because of my selfishness.

As you grow up you will understand that there are things in this life which we cannot control. Sometimes we cannot do or act as we wish just because it is what we want.

Dear baby, I think of you many, many times a day. Sometimes my heart is burdened and I feel guilty because I wronged you. But other times I imagine your happy smiling face and I am pleasantly surprised. Even in the future, when you grow up, you may not understand my mixed feelings.

I hope that you will be a member of a good family and that you will be loved, as well as healthy and strong. I will always pray for you and you will always remain in my heart. Eat well, sleep well, and play well. If in the future we do meet, I hope that we will not be ashamed of each other. Good-bye, my baby.

From your mother, who has wronged you

"*I* hope you will grow up full of life like a pine tree."

My son,

I don't know how to begin. You might be grown up when you read this letter. Yet I would prefer that you didn't read this letter because I worry about your pain and shock when you learn the truth about your birth and your birth mother.

I love you. Even though I repeat these words over and over, I know they are not enough. More than saying I love you, I should say I am sorry. My son! Can you forgive me? When I first saw you after your birth, it was as if I had loved you for a long time. When I looked at you, there were so many things I wanted to say to you. But the only thing I could do was cry without stopping. After that, I felt so much guilt because I couldn't do anything for you and I had to let you go. I wonder if you can understand that I had to let you go because I loved you and wanted you to be raised in a better environment.

How can I ask for your understanding and forgiveness? The fact that I gave birth to you and then placed you with others will leave deep scars on my heart forever. I hope that you won't suffer any great hurt because of me, and that this letter won't upset you. I want your life to be trouble-free.

I will always pray for you. I will think about you when I look up to the sky because you also look up to the sky. I feel so sorry that I had to say good-bye to you when you weren't conscious of anything, could barely move your hands and feet, and could not yet express your thoughts. That I was the one to send you away like that leaves me feeling heartbroken.

I hope you will grow up full of life like a pine tree.

Always be happy.

Your birth mother

P.S. Dear adoptive parents,

How do you do? I am the birth mother of your baby. I don't know how I can adequately express my thanks to you for raising the child to whom I gave birth. I guess I can only say thank you. I believe you will be good parents. I hope this baby will grow up to be an upright and normal person like others.

The birth father has the same last name as mine. He was twenty-four, one year older than me. He was a cheerful and sociable man. I thought we truly loved each other, but he just up and left me. Although I was happy about my baby when he was first born, I cried every day because I felt sad and guilty at not being able to give happiness to my child. I could hardly bear the thought of having been betrayed by my lover and having to let my first baby go.

I would really like to meet my baby someday, but I am afraid that he won't want to meet me because of his resentment and hatred toward me. Moreover, if meeting him should be a cause of trouble to others, I won't try to meet him.

Please lead my baby to be a righteous and happy person.

I want him to know God. Please love my baby.

Thank you very much.

"*Is* it possible that we will meet again?"

To my daughter,

I feel too unworthy to write this letter. I have looked back over my twenty-four years, and I can see how the time passed so fruitlessly. The past cannot be changed. Why did I live my life like that? Was it because I was unfeeling? Or was I a person with too weak a will? Although I regret it, it is like crying over spilled milk.

A baby born without blessing is ill-omened. I am a poor mother who could not hug you warmly, not even once. From conception to birth, so many thoughts and pains arise. I was so busy deceiving others that I sometimes even deceived myself, but I had to wait for nine months.

Why did I have to live like that, putting up with times that were unbearable? I even thought that death might bring peace to my heart. Is it human nature to care for life or is it the knowledge that life is the creation of God?

I bore you and sent you away. Even animals keep and raise their offspring. I hope that through this letter, you will someday understand my heart. It is the heart of a woman who bore a child in pain but had to send her away after birth, not being able to raise her, not even for a moment. It's like a scene from a novel.

Seeing your face after your first bath, I thought it miraculous that you looked just like me. They say blood is thicker than water . . . I was such a worthless mother—I could not breast-feed my baby even once. My daughter, please forgive me!

Was it perhaps God's plan? My life will be filled with yearning for you all the time. Is it possible that we will meet again?

Finally, something I can earnestly do for you: pray for your good health and proper development.

I await the unknown time when I might see you again.

"*I* call your name quietly in my heart."

My dear baby!

I am not able to imagine what you look like. Yes, I was not able to see you. If I had seen and hugged you, I would not have been able to send you away.

But I want to imagine how you look—your eyes, nose, mouth, hands, feet, head, everything. I sigh, and sigh again.

My heart can neither laugh nor cry. The song that I used to sing for you and the heart with which I used to wait for you, all those are worthless now without you. This time in which we cannot be together is nothing but painful for me. Just sitting here, missing you, my eyes fill with my tears without my realizing it.

I cannot see nor touch you, my dear baby, so I call your name quietly in my heart. Although you are not here with me now, I miss you very much, my beautiful flower. You will always be loved in my heart. You are clearer than a lotus flower, brighter than morning dew, and prettier than a rose, my beautiful flower!

The first thing that I want to tell you is that I am sorry and that I love you. I would really like to see you. I wanted to raise you by my own hand and in my own bosom.

I am sorry!

Finally, I want you to be happy with your parents who will raise you better than I could. I hope and pray for you with folded hands.

"*At* the place where you should be there is emptiness."

To my precious baby,

My child! The stars are especially bright tonight.

As I look up through the darkness at the stars, I write this letter to you, wherever you may be in this world. Is it to hide my tears that I have already started to like the dark?

What can I say to you, as a mother who is full of guilt? I am a mother without the right to be a mother. I don't think there is anything to be said except that I am sorry. I am even ashamed of the hand that is writing this letter. I just want to hide.

Dear baby! The stars are beautiful tonight. Just as the night comes to us, so the morning has already come to me.

Everything else remains the same; only your mother changes. At the place where you should be there is emptiness, and this empty spot in my heart is too big for anyone to fill.

The emptiness! The feeling of missing you! The heartbreak! Must I have these guilt–laden feelings as a mother?

Dear baby! Please forgive your mother who had to send you away. And please remember that this is the best way that I could have shown my love for you.

During the nine months of caring for you in my womb, I tried to give you all the love that should be given in your whole life. I prayed every day to the Virgin Mary that I would bear a healthy child, and that my child would grow up in a family full of love.

You already may have become a mature adult by the time you read this letter. Have you grown up beautifully and gracefully? Ah! I want to see you because I miss you so much.

Dear baby! Please grow up to become successful and happy. Remember that life is like a rocky road and you must be strong.

"*It was you who taught me not to hate this world.*"

Hello, my child!

It is a sunny afternoon and it seems the whole world is at peace.

I have wondered if I might meet you face to face someday, but I'm glad to meet you through this letter. I feel at a loss, frustrated, mixed up . . .

Our life together was really too short for us to say good-bye. I was so sad not to be called mother by you, and not to be able to give you the warmth of my love. People are so proud of delivering a baby boy and are so happy about it, as if they own the sky and the earth. However, I could not hold on to my happiness, as I had to let you go right after your birth. One thing I can do now is pray to see you again someday. There is nothing I can say if you think bad things about me when you become an adult. Life is a struggle, full of conflicts and the effort to maintain relationships with others.

I wonder if I can express for you the sorrow and the happiness of my pregnancy. Can you understand why I had to place you with others, although I wanted to keep you?

I know it is difficult for you to understand and accept me. I also had a very hard time when I decided to place you for adoption.

My baby . . . I can't stop crying while writing this letter because the image of your little body haunts my mind. I miss you so much.

How I wished to be your mother! How I wished to give my mothering to you. How bitter it is not to see your beautiful face each day of my life. That you, my flesh and blood, might be standing right next to me and I wouldn't even recognize you—how can I cope with such a fate?

My precious baby! It was you who taught me not to hate this world, and my love for you helped me overcome my desolate feelings and despair. Yet I could not keep you and was increasingly lonely after saying good-bye to you. I felt as if a piece of my heart had been painfully torn away. I cry just to think of you. Weak as my heart is, I think of your little cries and movements and pray unceasingly for you.

How scared, worried, and sad I was when I went through the process of your adoption, including giving up parental rights with the social worker at the adoption agency.

My sweetheart, can you forgive me? I am writing this letter because I want you to know what happened in your life. Your mother is also sad, with a deep wound in her heart.

My boy! Stay healthy. I hope you will be warm and considerate to others. Try to see the bright side of this world. And be a person who starts again rather than one who gives up when you fail.

Always thinking of you.

$\mathcal{C}$hristian faith

Koreans bring to their religious faith the same personal and
emotional intensity they bring to other parts of their lives.
Ae Ran Won is a Christian agency, and religious instruction is
part of its educational program. This is not unusual for Korea,
where the church is a significant presence; 25 percent of the
population actively practices Christianity. Some of the birth
mothers write that they have found restoration and peace in
Christian faith, and seek forgiveness as a way to unburden their
deep guilt. They admit shame and guilt, but hold on to grace
and hope for both themselves and their birth children.

"*I wasn't even able to give you a name.*"

My darling baby,

I don't know what to say to you, and I wonder where and how I should start . . .

I wasn't even able to give you a name or respond to the beautiful smile that you showed me when we met for the first time. You are already gone from my bosom. I am ashamed to use the word mother, but can I show this mother's love to you?

How can I show that you did not make me miserable or sad while you were in my body? All you did was change places from my body into this world; there is no change in my love and thanks toward you.

I gave you your body, but God gave you your soul. I strongly believe God will lead your life forever.

I wonder if we will have a chance to meet again in the long years ahead. How can you greet me, and with what words? Will you reproach me by saying, "Why did you abandon me?" Or will you comfort me in a mature manner?

I am truly anxious about that, but won't make excuses to you. Rather, I want to make clear that the pain we suffered as an unwed mother and as an adopted baby couldn't be changed.

Neither can our circumstances take away the dignity and the aims of our lives. Rather, those pains can lead us closer to God.

Now I know the only thing that this mother can do for you is pray. I will pray for you no matter where I am.

My sweetheart, please remember that there is one person who will keep praying for you even though you can't see her, and that person is your birth mother.

God keep you now and forever.

"*I* will never forget your eyes, now and forever."

How can I begin?

You are my baby. My darling baby! It has been almost a month since I said good-bye to you.

It was a painful but happy time when you were in my body for nine months. You were born in September, and your mother (I hesitate to use this word) was so impressed to see you for the first time. When I turned my head to see your face right after your birth, I could see your eyes.

Your eyes were just opened when I saw you, and they were so clear and pure. Your eyes were so wonderful and marvelous. It was just for two seconds, but I will never forget your eyes, now and forever.

My darling Jin . . .

I named you Jin using the name in my diary. I kept a diary
when I was young and I always started it by writing, "My loving
Jin." From that time on, the name Jin became a part of me and
when my baby was born, I named the baby Jin. That baby is
you. There were other reasons to name you Jin. The meaning of
the word "jin" is *truth,* and I wanted you to be a trustworthy
person. Also, Jin was the generational name of your uncle.

I wonder how you will grow up. Even though I can't be beside
you and watch you grow up, I am not worried about it. I trust
that God, who is always with me, will be with you forever.

When I placed you with others I had one hope. That hope was,
"Although I cannot meet you in this world, I can meet you in
heaven." However, I can't stop missing you until I see you.

Jin . . . my darling baby.

Good-bye.

I pray for you, and whatever anyone may say, I am proud of
being your mother. I love you more than anyone else.

You resemble me a lot. Stay healthy until I can meet you again.
I love you.

"_P_lease take care and be a
good son to your parents."

My dear child,

The winter has passed, and the warm sunshine indicates that
spring has come. You could not yet feel any sense of time or
season, yet I could feel the mystery of the greatness of life as I
watched you crying. I am very sorry that I cannot raise you,
even though I want to. I feel like I have committed such a big
sin against you by giving birth to you in this corrupt world.

I felt no resentment as I went through labor pains. I asked God,
my grandmother, and you for forgiveness. I realized why people
seek God when they experience agony and pain. It is because
God is the Father of all of us. I went to church every Sunday up
until I was fifteen years old, but I did not have a sincere faith.
I attended church only half-heartedly, and as a result started

going in the wrong direction. I liked this world more than God. I liked listening to my friends more than the Word of God.

Following that lifestyle, I met your father. There was a big age gap, but we loved each other. Your father did not want to have a child due to the circumstances. I thought that it would be very difficult to raise you by myself, so I decided to send you to an adoption agency. I thought it would be better for you to grow up in a good environment with nice parents. I hoped you could be raised in Korea because then you could grow up without knowing about your adoption.

You resembled your father so much with your curly hair, and you were the prettiest baby ever! If you were to come to see me, I wonder what you would look like.

I hope you will become a nice man, but above all, I want you to be a Christian. I have three wishes for you. I want you to live with the Word of God, respect your parents, and have a proper sense of values. These are the promises between you and me.

My child, pray when you encounter difficulties, and God will help you. I will pray for you and me. I know God will forgive me. I want to make a new beginning. My child, let us do it together. As your mother I will live decently, and as my son you will be a good man.

Dear child, please take care and be a good son to your parents. Bye.

From your mother

"*I* wonder if you still look like your daddy."

My beloved baby,

Your mother wants to ask your forgiveness through this letter because I cannot meet you face-to-face. I wonder how old you might be when you read this letter. I am writing with the hope and a prayer to God that I can help you understand me better.

It is daybreak, and rain is falling outside. I wonder if you still look like your daddy. You had big eyes with double eyelids, a big nose, and lips moving as if they were sucking on something. You were not like a newborn baby and, as I looked at you, I hated myself enough to want to die. I couldn't hold you because I was scared. I couldn't breathe because of the reality that I couldn't raise you.

Listen carefully, my baby, because this is very hard for me to tell. Your father disclaimed you. When I became pregnant, your daddy was a student and we were not a married couple. He thought that if we could not take responsibility for you, it would be better for all three of us if I did not give birth to you. I thought he was so heartless and I truly wanted to die.

As time went on (I was trying to hide the pregnancy in my small body), I realized that he would not come back to me, and it might be better not to give birth to you. However, God loved us. Whenever I thought of having an abortion, God let you wriggle and let me feel that you were alive in my body. And then, you were born.

Your daddy disclaimed you, and your mother used you as an excuse to get your daddy back! How unfeeling we were to you! I also suffered from my inability to raise you after your birth.

How dearly I wanted to raise you . . .

How dearly I wanted to hold you . . .

I thought I could not live after letting you go. How I wished to keep you in my body rather than give birth to you.

As time goes on, memory fades away, but I think you are with me as far as my memory of the night you and I spent together. I feel forgetfulness is one of the tremendous blessings God gave us. I forgave your daddy. I forgave myself for letting you go. And I decided to stand alone to meet your coming home day—I wonder if this day will come or not—with a happy face, and to be a mommy you can be proud of. Can you understand that?

I am praying for you to be a wise person. Be a person who can stand firmly in God and invite God into the core of your heart. The only thing I can do for you is pray, and I feel grateful to God for letting me do this for you.

It is almost morning, and it is still raining outside. I am thankful to God for the courage to talk about my life to you. Life is hard. But with God's love, life is not all tough. Have strength, my darling, and don't forget a big smile.

I love you now and forever!

Your mom
100 days after your birth

"*I give to you all of my love.*"

My dear baby,

The year is already half over, and now it is summer. My baby! I am very anxious to know how you are doing. I wonder if you and your family are all right.

My darling, as your birth mother I am ashamed and sorry that I could not show you the warm affection I had for you. It was so difficult to have to let you go within a day after your birth. I can hardly find the right words to express my sadness. Can you imagine how my heart must have felt to place with others the child to whom I had given birth?

Oh my child! If you ask why I gave birth to a child I couldn't raise, I have no explanation at all. My situation was miserable when I was pregnant. I was inexperienced and not yet ready to raise a child. Although I was pregnant, I had to work from morning till night. But even then, there was no money left over. I also didn't know where the rest of my family was. I wanted to forget that I was pregnant.

Eight months have passed since I delivered you and things have changed. I am staying at Ae Ran Won, where I have learned to play the piano. I'm also learning things like flower arranging, Oriental embroidery for hanbok, Chinese writing, and typing.

The most important thing is that I have found God's love through Bible study and worship. Now I pray for you every day. Before your birth, I didn't know what parental love was, and I sometimes resented my own parents. Now I have found what parental love is and I don't regret that I gave birth to you.

I decided that placing you for adoption was better for you than suffering from hunger and poverty with me. I thought you could be happy if you met wonderful parents through adoption. I do not regret my decision. I always pray that you will know God's love and be happy and wise. I pray that you will be spiritually happy, place others' well-being ahead of your own, thank and glorify the Lord, and share your love with your neighbors.

Sweetheart! Although there is nothing I can give you, I give to you all of my love. Stay in good health. Good-bye.

Your loving mom.

P.S. Dear adoptive parents,

Is my baby grown up now? I guess you have given her a name. Thinking of God's grace given to me and my baby, I call her Grace. Please love this baby as if you had given birth to her and lead her to know God's love.

Help this child to overcome difficulties through prayer. I also pray for your love and the well-being of your family. Please take good care of Grace.

Good-bye,

Grace's birth mom

"*My heart was melted by your precious life.*"

To my cute and lovely baby,

I am writing to you because I sent you so far away, yet have so much to tell you. I don't know where to begin. I imagine there are many things that you want to know. You probably want to know where and how you were born, why you had to be adopted to a different country, and who your birth parents are.

Your mom was raised in a small country village as an innocent girl. With my one older brother, two older sisters, and one younger brother, we five siblings were a happy family who loved each other and obeyed and respected our parents. After my high school graduation in June, I came to Seoul and started to work. Then I met your father at work and became pregnant. Your dad is a nice person who is full of love.

But my baby, I believe that it was God who planned your life on this earth. God loved my soft heart and allowed me to give new birth and life to you. Now I am thankful to Him for giving me a chance to do so. I also believe that God will take care of you, and live my life in prayer that He will do so.

Do you know how you were born? You were born with a loud cry that woke up the morning quiet at 1:30 A.M. When I heard your cry, I momentarily forgot the labor pain and started to cry out of pure joy. When I saw you again, you were sleeping so peacefully, maybe because it was too hard to come into the world. Then I started to pray again that God would guide your life in His love and take you as His child.

When I learned I was pregnant, I was shocked. I was confused and had many struggles. I lost my desire and aspiration to live in this world, and it was extremely difficult. The biggest difficulty was the fact that this society would not forgive me. I quit my job, started to live alone without contact with my family, and went to a place called Ae Ran Won—a home for unmarried mothers. Now I am thankful and believe that it was God's wish.

I got to know God, and met Christ at Ae Ran Won. I realized your importance. Although at first I had felt ashamed and guilty that I was pregnant, I no longer felt that way after I came to Ae Ran Won. It made me realize what a precious baby you were. I love you, my baby, and my love for you cannot be exchanged with anything in this world. You who were born with the blessing of the Lord are very important to me. That is why I "gave you" to the Lord and want the Lord to bless and take care of you as His child.

I am thankful to God and His wondrous power that He has provided you a very happy family and good parents to raise you. I also am thankful that I can talk to you and watch you growing up. I hope and pray that, as you grow, you will come to respect and obey the Lord and your parents, and that you will be a healthy boy.

I promise you that your mom is going to work hard as a member of this society and live my life as a good Christian who obeys God and seeks first the kingdom of God. At last, I want you to know that my heart was melted by your precious life, and I love you very much.

Good-bye.

Your beautiful mom

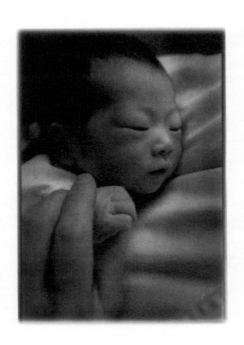

$\mathcal{M}$emories and the future

Adopted people and their families might wonder what the future brings for women who once resided at Ae Ran Won. Mrs. Han, Director of Ae Ran Won, shared a few stories with us (using pseudonyms):

> Ms. Kim, who gave birth to her baby in 1990, has since gone on for further educational training with a scholarship from Ae Ran Won. She met her husband through her work, and has shared with him her experience as a birth mother—a difficult thing to do in Korea. Her husband understands and accepts this part of her life. Ms. Kim struggled with emotions of grief and guilt for a while, but with follow-up counseling at Ae Ran Won she has gradually come to terms with her feelings.

> With Ae Ran Won's help, Ms. Lee found a job after choosing adoption for her child in 1994. She married a couple of years later, and now has another baby boy. Ms. Lee still keeps in touch with a few friends from Ae Ran Won, but does not feel she can tell her husband about who they are or about her first child. Because of the stigma of pregnancy outside of marriage, she fears this information would destroy her family. She believes she made the best decision for her first birth child, but misses him deeply.

Ms. Kwon carried her baby to term in 1996 despite great pressure from her boyfriend and mother. As a result of her decision she lost many family and school relationships, but with scholarship money from Ae Ran Won she has immersed herself once again in finishing her college degree. Ms. Kwon has no regrets about her adoption decision, but continues to wrestle with lingering grief and loss.

This brief glance into the continuing experiences of a few birth mothers conveys some of the same complicated feelings of loss and hope encountered in these letters. Some women write that the birth of their children seemed destined, and others express the hope that destiny will bring them together once again. While in many cases a face-to-face reunion is not possible, these letters make it clear that many women hold tight to the memories of their children. Above all, they hope and pray that their children will have a bright future.

"*I want you to be a happy person with a big smile.*"

My dear baby,

What a great joy it was to hear that I was pregnant! But that joy was short-lived, for I started to ask myself many questions. What can I do for my baby? How will my baby feel about the decision I am now making? How will it affect my baby? I cannot help but think about these things.

I was afraid and trembled at the thought of becoming a mother at the age of twenty. You were in my body for nine months, but I could not live with you after your birth.

Whenever I see babies, they remind me of you, and then I cry. I imagine you in my heart and think that you are somewhere else since I gave birth to you. Our very short first and last meeting, right after your birth, is still vivid in my heart and makes me cry. I thought that letting you go was the best decision for you. However, I couldn't forget your face after seeing you, and I even regretted that I had become pregnant.

Now I have only one wish, and that is for you to be happy with your adoptive parents. This is my life-long prayer. I want you to be a happy person with a big smile. Be a good Christian. I did wrong to you, but I trust God will keep you safe.

My darling baby! Even though you are so far away from me, you are always deep in my heart. Your presence in this world makes me happy.

My sweet baby! I've learned a lot from you, like what real love is and how precious life is. This doesn't mean that I'd exchange these lessons for you. I hope I can see you someday, although if we do meet, we should do so with other people around us.

My darling, I hope you can remember that there is one woman who prays for you—the very woman who gave birth to you.

Good-bye.

"*I* cannot give up my wish to see you again."

To my baby,

My child! I used to wake up in the middle of the night, as if I heard your crying. But it was only a dream, and you were not there. I then cried because I missed you so much. Now I have learned how to express my sorrow without crying. I have cried deep down in my heart with my yearning for you.

My heart was pierced with sorrow at not seeing you again, and your image has become clearer and clearer in my heart. Your pure face . . . your shapely nose . . . your lips moving as if they were sucking on something . . . and your expression when you cried. You who were so adorable, my baby.

My heart is broken because I cannot see you again, and my longing becomes deeper each day. I cannot give up my wish to see you. I will never forget you, and I will wonder about you. Can I ever forgive myself for letting you go? It seems I cannot.

My honey, I am sorry I couldn't give anything to you. I wanted to buy pretty clothes for you, feed you, change your diapers, and look after you when you were sick. But I couldn't do anything for you, and that made me so sad.

Is it possible to say I loved you, even though I couldn't keep you and instead placed you with others? How I wish to see you again! If I am lucky enough to see you again in the future, I will show my heartfelt love for you. Is this an impossible wish? However slim the chance, I do hope to see you.

My darling, you looked exactly like your daddy! As you grow up, might you wonder about why I had to let you go, and then reproach me? Will you see it as merely an excuse if I say I let you go because I loved you?

Your mother . . . I was twenty-one when I got pregnant. I was a college student majoring in accounting. I was an unwed mother with no financial independence. I was supported by my parents and didn't know what life was really like. I had no money to support you, and no self-confidence about parenting. Also, I had to finish school.

It was foolish, but I often cried as I watched my stomach becoming large with you, since I couldn't tell my parents and friends that I was pregnant.

I was scared to live my life as an unwed mother, so I decided to let you go. Four hours of labor pains made me so attached to you, and I can never forget your first look . . . I loved you so much, and all my heart was yours. To have to accept that I couldn't live with you was the hardest moment of my life.

My child! What can I do for you now? The only thing this guilty mom can do for you is pray. I pray for you every day: "God, please let my baby be happy with his new parents. Help him to not suffer from the sorrow which I caused him. Help him to be emotionally healthy!"

My darling! I hope you'll be loved by others. I hope you can take care of others and love yourself. I hope you can thank God for the smallest things, and think that everything that is given to you is a blessing. I hope you'll be brave and courageous, and do your best in your duties.

My dear child, I believe God listened to my prayer and will be with you now and forever. Good-bye.

Your mother

"*You were like an angel who had come from heaven.*"

Dear baby,

When I call your name, I cannot call you "my darling" or "my baby." I don't think you can understand my feelings because you are so young, but I feel so guilty that I didn't give you enough love. And so I want to share this story with you.

When I met you for the first time, I noticed that your skin was so clean and white, and you seldom cried. I was so delighted and enchanted by you that I completely forgot that we soon had to say good-bye. I couldn't hug you when you looked at me with your beautiful black eyes since you were such a little baby and looked frail, and I regret that.

My baby! Your mother still doesn't feel like she actually gave birth to you. The moment of your birth came after a long and painful labor, and is still so clear in my mind. But you were so adorable, I still can't believe that you are my daughter. You were like an angel who had come from heaven, and I can never forget you. I miss you so much.

I keep a diary for recalling each day, and write about you in my diary every day. I always pray for your health and your future. And that is the only thing I can do for you now.

My baby! I am very curious and anxious about your future. Your future is more important to me than my own. I trust you will meet every circumstance very well. God is between you and me, and I trust that He will certainly connect us with an invisible string. I met God during the nine months of my pregnancy. I was born anew and could start a new life with my love for you. You gave me a lot, for which I am grateful. My baby, I love you.

"*Know that your spirit is within my spirit.*"

To my adorable baby,

When you were first born, your mother was extremely happy. Your eyes were wide open, like two clear lakes. I remember vividly how when I hugged you, you yawned in my arms.

My loving child, I wonder what you are doing right now. I am sorry that I cannot be next to you. It has been almost a month since you were born. I hope you will understand why I had to give you up.

My heart aches that I cannot live with you, but wherever you are and whatever you do, I hope you will live your life to the best of your ability. I also hope you will develop your strengths and use your abilities, so that people will be proud of you.

Live courageously. I will also try to live my life the best way that I can so that I may be a role model to you, if only in spirit. If we do meet again in the future, I hope we will not be disappointed by each other.

Even though I had you in my arms for only a short while, I thought of many things. Would you be hurt because of my irresponsibility? Would you be able to find good adoptive parents? Would you truly be a well-adjusted person?

Many questions and thoughts have burdened my heart about this situation. I took these thoughts and considerations into my heart as I chose your name. Your name means *big and bright*. My hope is that you will live up to your name, and shine brightly over a vast area.

We are not apart. Know that your spirit is within my spirit and that even if we are not in the same place, our spirits are together. As we live our different lives and things get too tough, let us each look up at the stars and talk to each other.

I will always pray for you. Let us live our lives to the best of our abilities.

Good-bye, my loving child.

"*My* precious baby!
Sleep soundly."

My precious love!

Rain is wetting the ground to greet the spring. A pleasant breeze brushes the tip of my nose. A day like today would be even more beautiful if I could hold you in my arms and watch the trees swaying in the wind.

I do not have much to say to you. I can tell you about the joy and excitement that I felt on the day you were born, as well as the tears of sorrow and pain.

Although I waited nine months as if it were only a day, sadness and sorrow instead of joy, regret and fear instead of hope, rose up from deep within my heart.

I had to forget the joy of your birth in just a few minutes, and then we had to forget one another. I had to send you away without being prepared for how to say good-bye.

My precious love! I wanted to give you so much love, and I still regret that I was not able to.

If only I could have held you in my arms . . . If only I could have held your hand . . . If only I could have touched your skin to remember a little bit of what it feels like.

I just wanted to keep you right next to me and hold you with my love. But I was afraid of holding you. No, I was afraid of sending you away. Dear baby! You are a creation of God and also a life that was planned by God. Therefore, I loved you even more and was deeply hurt in my heart.

When I lie down and close my eyes, I remember when you were just born. I also remember you crying in your blanket.

Dear baby! I will always remember the love in my heart that belongs to you, even after I die. I just want you to grow up and be happy. Although I will not be able to see you with my eyes, just imagining it fills my heart with joy.

My precious baby! Sleep soundly.

With regret that I am not able to tell the whole story.

"*I* love you from far away."

A letter to my baby,

It seems like only yesterday that spring was coming with the strong scent of flowers in the air . . . now August is almost over and much-needed rain is on the way. I miss you and long to see you. It has been almost a month since I saw you and heard your cries. Sometimes when I hold your photo and look at it intently it makes me long for you even more.

My wish for you is that you will have a healthy smile and will receive much love from many people. I hope you don't find me too presumptuous in referring to myself as your mother.

Seoul, Korea, where you were born, is a place of blue skies. Although under that sky there is much pain that is beyond our understanding, there are many beautiful people here. They initially gave us comfort, but now you are no longer here but in a foreign land, the United States. I hope that you will be happy, that you will grow up receiving respect as an individual, and that you will have a good life. Even though you may blame me and hate me for giving you up, I hope you do not think that I did this willingly or easily.

I hope that you are being brought up by adoptive parents who have warm and kind hearts . . . never forget to be grateful for them. Be always obedient to them.

Another wish that I want to leave with you is that you may have the gift of wisdom. I hope that people will laugh and be comforted and share love because of you and your kind heart. I also hope that despite your cute and gentle name that you will be a strong child—strong and disciplined toward yourself but gentle toward others.

I love you from far away, even having only seen you for a little while. I will always think of you and pray for you. I love you.

Your mother

About Ae Ran Won
Provided by Mrs. Han Sang-soon, Director

Background

Ae Ran Won is a home for unwed mothers that has grown and developed over the last forty years. House of Grace, the forerunner of Ae Ran Won, was established in April of 1960 as a home for runaway girls and prostitutes. Its founder, an American Presbyterian missionary named Eleanor E. Van Lierop, ran the home herself and supported it entirely through private donations.

In 1973, House of Grace became a home for unwed mothers. One reason for the change was the growing desire of the Korean government to establish facilities that responded to the needs of these young women. A second reason was that at the time, there were many children abandoned on the street who simply did not survive. It was found that these babies had been abandoned by unwed mothers who could not find anyone to help them.

In 1983, when Eleanor Van Lierop retired and returned to America, House of Grace was turned over to the charitable work foundation of the General Assembly of the Presbyterian Church of Korea. It was subsequently named Ae Ran Won in honor of Mrs. Van Lierop. Her Korean name was Ae Ran, meaning "Planting Love." That same year Ae Ran Won was recognized by the government as a home for unwed mothers, and has since then received some financial support from the government.

Services

Many Korean people think that an unmarried pregnant woman should decide on abortion. Without asking the expectant mother, most parents also prefer that their unwed daughters have an abortion. When an unwed mother decides to give birth, she has to sacrifice many things—job, school, friends and sometimes even family. Thus these women desperately need help.

Ae Ran Won's overall objective is to provide services to meet the physical, emotional, financial, and spiritual needs of our residents. Ae Ran Won has developed a program of professional individual and group counseling, medical care, emotional and sex education, vocational training, and other related services. One of our goals is to help young women decide whether they will try to care for their babies or make an adoption plan for them. We also help the young women plan for their own futures. About 85 percent of the birth mothers choose adoption, but after making that decision they often experience guilt, loss, and despair.

Ae Ran Won is dedicated to sharing the love of Christ by serving these women. We try to introduce the Gospel to them during their stay. If they accept Jesus as their Lord and Savior, they can choose to be baptized.

Ae Ran Won Today

Ae Ran Won has ten suites, each of which can accommodate four women, for a total of forty residents. There is also a central kitchen, a dining room, a library, an exercise room, a lounge, bathrooms, and counseling facilities. We accept unmarried and pregnant women as our residents.

We are fortunate to have twenty-five volunteers, who along with our staff of seven provide essential services to the residents. There is no charge to the residents. Ae Ran Won is a nonprofit organization, with a portion of the funding provided by the Korean government, and the rest provided by church and private donations.

The number of unwed mothers who request assistance from Ae Ran Won has increased steadily. There were 150 in 1990, 203 in 1995, and 249 in 1997. As a result, our present resources and budget are not adequate to meet the residents' needs. Ae Ran Won does not want merely to provide these women with food and shelter during a time of crisis and then send them on their way. We want to equip them with the tools they need to be self-sufficient and productive members of society. We want to help them not only while they are in residence, but also after they leave and are trying to make it on their own. In some cases, there is a need for follow-up services.

We need your prayers and donations for our program and its development. We would be grateful for any donations you wish to make to Ae Ran Won's ongoing work. Our address is:

Ae Ran Won
127-20 Daeshin-Dong
Sudaemun-Gu
Seoul, South Korea 120-160

Thank you.

Acknowledgments

The editor wishes to acknowledge the exceptional support and input of Maynard Dorow, Shirley Dorow, and Michael Wilt, as well as the considerable contributions of Maxine Walton, Jeff Mondloh, Martha Vickery, Stephen Wunrow, Pat Johnston, Jane Brown, Hyun-sook Han, and Marietta Spencer. For invaluable assistance with design and production, my thanks to Kim Dalros and Stephanie Billecke. A debt of gratitude is owed to the many people who undertook the painstaking task of translating these letters, including Bae Kyung-hee, Kim Min-sook, Park Hyun-min, Chung Ma-ree, Lee Min-kyo, and Chen Suh Yoon. Also, my appreciation to the artist of the wonderful painting on the cover, Kim Soo-ik, for sharing his talent. Special thanks to Kim, Tim, and Leah for speaking frankly. Finally, a hearty salute to Brian Boyd of Yeong & Yeong Book Company and to Mrs. Han Sang-soon, Director of Ae Ran Won: their broad vision and thoughtful perseverance brought this project to fruition.

About the Contributors

Sara Dorow lived all of her childhood in South Korea and later worked for several years as an administrator of Chinese and Korean adoption programs. She is also the author of *When You Were Born in China*. Ms. Dorow holds an M.A. in East Asian Studies and is currently pursuing a Ph.D. in Sociology.

Han Sang-soon has a B.A. in Social Work from Ewha Woman's University in Seoul. She has worked at the Christian Adoption Program and Holt Children's Services, and has been the Director of Ae Ran Won for more that eight years. During this time she has overseen the steady expansion of Ae Ran Won's unique programs of outreach and support for unwed mothers in Korea. Mrs. Han is a devoted Christian and a passionate worker dedicated to the birth mothers who come to Ae Ran Won.

Maxine Walton and **Jeff Mondloh** are Licensed Social Workers on the staff of the Post Adoption Services Department at Children's Home Society of Minnesota. Both have extensive experience providing counseling and other support services to internationally adopted persons of all ages and their families.

Kim Soo-ik graduated from Hong Ik School of Art and Kyung Hee University. His art is well known in Korea and throughout Asia, due to many awards and private exhibitions since 1976. He is currently a professor of art at several Korean universities.

Stephen Wunrow contributed his photography to two earlier books from Yeong & Yeong Book Company: *When You Were Born in Korea* and *When You Were Born in China*. Together with his wife Martha Vickery, he publishes *Korean Quarterly,* a magazine that covers topics of Korean interest. His photos on pages 13, 14, 34, 55, 94, and 123 were taken at Ae Ran Won.